NF 551.21/G   17420   £10.99

17420

CLOSER LOOK AT

VOLCANOES

Jen Green

Franklin Watts
LONDON ● SYDNEY

An Aladdin Book

© Aladdin Books Ltd 1996
Designed and produced by
Aladdin Books Ltd
28 Percy Street
London W1P 0LD

First published in Great Britain
in 1996 by
Franklin Watts
96 Leonard Street
London EC2A 4RH

A catalogue record for this book is available from the
British Library

ISBN: 0 7496 2470 1

Editor
Alex Edmonds

Designer
Gary Edgar-Hyde

Picture Research
Brooks Krikler Research

Front cover illustration
Gary Edgar-Hyde

Illustrators
Mike Saunders
Peter Kesteven
Aziz Khan
Ian Moores
David Russell

Certain illustrations have appeared in
earlier books created by Aladdin Books.

The consultant, Joyce Pope took her first degree in
geography. She has worked for many years as a lecturer
at the Natural History Museum, where she has studied
amongst many things, volcanoes. She now
specialises in biology.

CONTENTS

INTRODUCTION

An erupting volcano is an awesome sight. Red-hot lava, ash, rocks and steam shoot from a volcano's crater to transform a landscape in hours or even minutes. Erupting volcanoes cause devastation and environmental pollution. Even today, with modern technology at their disposal, scientists cannot accurately predict the time and scale of eruptions. Yet volcano ash fertilises the soil and provides energy as well as valuable gems and minerals.

olcanoes are eruptions of molten (melted) rock, called lava, and gases from deep inside the Earth. Volcanoes occur where the Earth's crust is weak enough to allow these hot materials to break through to the surface. Flows of lava and ash build up around the opening forming the mound of the volcano.

Hot rocks
Inside the crater of an active volcano is a seething cauldron of molten rock from deep inside the Earth.

Earth's skin
Our planet is not the same all the way through. It is made up of a number of different layers. The hard, outer layer is called the crust (right). This skin is relatively thin.

WHAT ARE

Crust

Mantle

Outer core

Inner core

INSIDE THE EARTH

Beneath the Earth's crust is an extremely hot layer of dense rock called the mantle (left). Inside the mantle is the core, made up of an outer layer of liquid metal, and a dense, inner core of solid metal alloys. Scientists believe the temperature at the Earth's core may be as high as 5,000 degrees Centigrade. Heating and cooling produced in the core cause slow-moving currents in the rock of the mantle. Molten rock, called magma, rises from the mantle to near the surface. As it reaches the surface of the volcano, magma becomes lava. Some forces its way through the crust to the surface, and this is what forms a volcano.

ON CLOSER INSPECTION – *VOLCANOES IN SPACE*

Volcanoes exist on other planets in our solar system too, including Mars and Venus. The largest yet discovered is Olympus Mons on Mars. The *Voyager* spacecraft took photographs of volcanoes erupting on Io (right), one of Jupiter's moons, in 1979.

VOLCANOES?

WHEN A VOLCANO ERUPTS

Magma from deep within the Earth's mantle rises and collects in a chamber near the surface where it mixes with gases and water. Pressure inside the Earth forces the magma to find a weak spot in the crust, and surge upwards through a central vent or chimney. Red-hot lava, gases, ash and steam erupt through the crater, a funnel-shaped opening at the top of the vent.

Cloud of ash and gas

Central vent

Lava

Cone

Side vent

Magma chamber

What shape?

Many volcanoes are cone-shaped with steep sides (top left), like Mount Fuji in Japan. Others, called shield volcanoes, are shaped like upturned saucers or shields (top right). An example of this type is Mauna Loa, Hawaii.

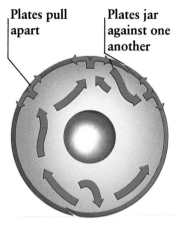

The Earth's crust feels solid. But scientists show that it is made up of a number of vast plates which fit together like giant paving stones. These plates float like rafts, on the Earth's upper mantle. Over millions of years, movements deep within the Earth cause the plates to drift slowly. Most volcanic activity occurs along the plate edges.

The mantle
Heat and pressure at the Earth's core cause currents to circulate in the mantle. This causes the plates to float on the mantle – they can move together or apart.

DRIFTING

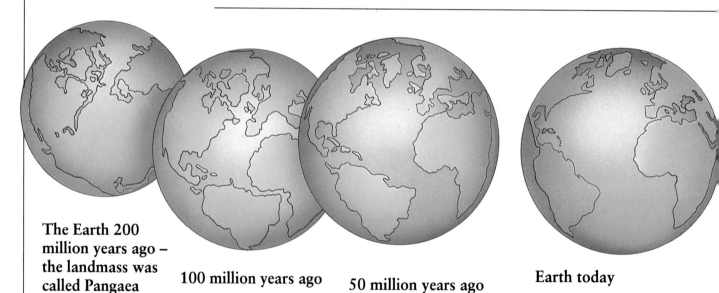

The Earth 200 million years ago – the landmass was called Pangaea

100 million years ago

50 million years ago

Earth today

CONTINENTAL DRIFT

The continents of the Earth have not always existed in their present positions. Scientists believe that 200 million years ago, all the land on Earth was joined together in a single land mass, a super-continent called Pangaea.

Over millions of years, movements within the Earth caused this land mass to break up and drift apart to form the seven continents we now know. The plates continue to drift today, and this is called continental drift.

ON CLOSER INSPECTION
– *Hotspots*

Unlike most volcanoes, hotspot volcanoes occur in the middle of plates. As the plate moves slowly above the hot spot over millions of years, a chain of volcanoes may form. An example is the chain of Hawaiian islands in the Pacific plate (right).

PLATES

One plate may carry both continent and ocean bed. It is the plates that move, not the continents.

The continent of Australia sits in the middle of a plate. There are no active volcanoes in Australia.

Ring of Fire
The map below shows the positions of the Earth's main plates, about 15 in all. The Earth's crust is weakest along the edges of the plates, which is why most volcanoes – and earthquakes – occur along these edges. Both earthquakes and volcanoes are common on the "Ring of Fire", round the rim of the Pacific plate. The theory of plate movement is called plate tectonics.

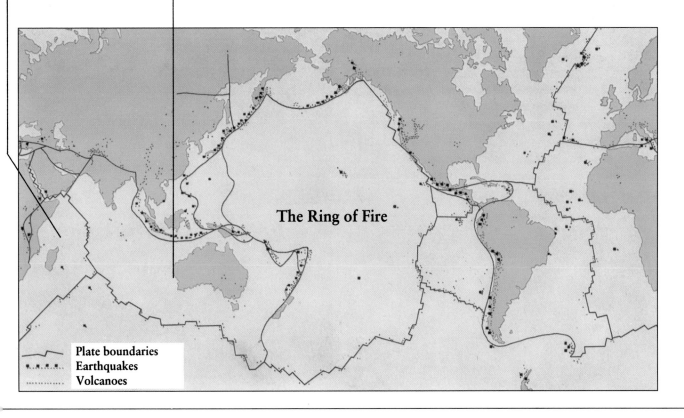

The Ring of Fire

———— Plate boundaries
.... Earthquakes
.... Volcanoes

Black smokers

On mid-ocean ridges, hot springs called black smokers are often found (below). Clouds of hot water, black with sulphur and other minerals, pour from these springs. Black smokers were first discovered in 1977. Many scientific surveys are now under way to examine them and the sea life that flourishes in the surrounding waters.

Many of the Earth's volcanoes are under the sea. The Earth's crust under the oceans is relatively thin, about 5 km, compared to the continental crust, which is between 30 and 60 km thick. Magma is able to force its way up through the thin crust, particularly at plate edges. The hot molten lava explodes when it hits the cold sea water, spewing out thick black clouds of ash and steam.

UNDERSEA

EXTINCT VOLCANOES

An atoll is a circle of coral around the edge of an extinct volcano. The atoll is formed from the hard skeletons of millions of tiny creatures that have since died. The volcano rims have usually been worn down by the sea, or sunk back under the water's surface.

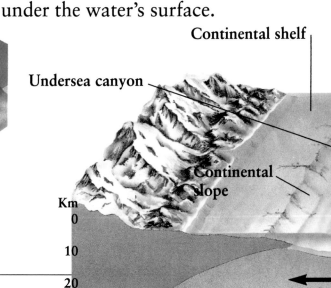

Continental shelf

Undersea canyon

Continental slope

Km
0

10

20

30

In November 1963, fishermen saw a great column of smoke and ash rise from the sea south-west of Iceland. The next day a new island appeared, and it continued to grow. The volcano, which was named Surtsey, had been caused by the Mid-Atlantic plates moving apart. Today it measures 2.6 sq km.

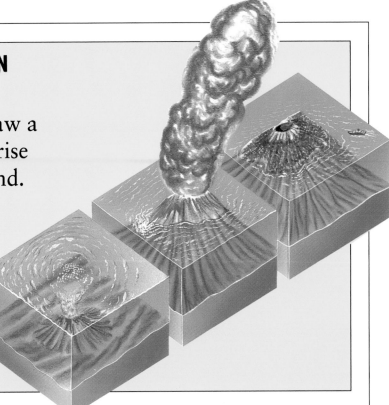

VOLCANOES

VOLCANIC RIFTS

Where plate edges occur in the middle of oceans, volcanic activity forms chains of undersea mountains cut by rift valleys. These rifts are caused as the plates slowly pull apart, causing a crack to develop. Magma wells up to fill the crack and then solidifies, forming a new strip of crust (a ridge) which grows wider. If an undersea eruption continues for long enough, a shield volcano may eventually build up to break the surface and form land.

Ocean trenches

When two old plates meet undersea, one dives beneath the other to form a deep ocean trench (below). The deepest is the Mariana Trench in the Pacific, 10,920 metres deep.

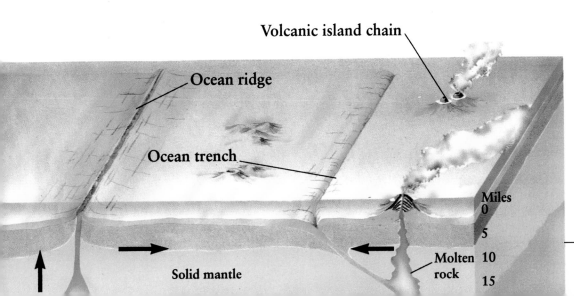

Volcanic island chain

Ocean ridge

Ocean trench

Miles
0

5

Molten 10
rock

Solid mantle

15

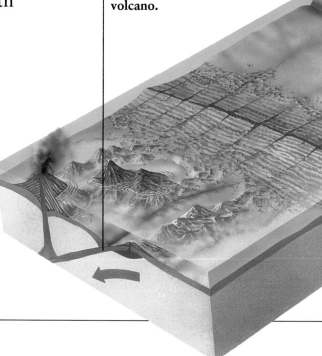

hen the plates forming our planet's crust drift together and collide, one slowly dives beneath the other. This process, called subduction, causes violent volcanic activity and geological upheaval. These plate collisions differ, depending whether they occur on land or at sea.

WHEN

Great Rift Valley

When two plates pull apart on land, the result is a rift valley with volcanoes along the edges of the rift. The Great Rift Valley in East Africa was formed in this way.

MOUNTAIN CHAINS

When an ocean plate collides with a continental plate, the ocean plate is forced down into the mantle, forming a trench. Some of the rocks that formed the ocean crust melt in the mantle to form magma. Under great heat and pressure they may be forced upwards again, to erupt in a line of volcanoes near the continent's edge. The spectacular Andes mountain chain in South America (below) is an example of this.

When two ocean plates meet, one is pushed down into the mantle, leaving a deep ocean trench. This plate melts and produces molten rock which may erupt as a volcano.

ON CLOSER INSPECTION
– *Clash of the Continents*

When continents collide, plates crumple together and are forced upwards to form a high mountain range. The Himalayan range, the highest mountains in the world, are relatively young mountains which are still rising.

PLATES COLLIDE

Mountain chains have formed at the edges of continents where two plates have collided.

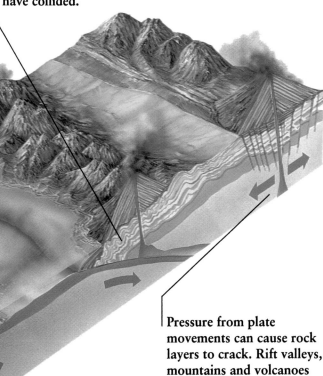

Pressure from plate movements can cause rock layers to crack. Rift valleys, mountains and volcanoes may then occur.

When two ocean plates pull apart, molten material rises up and solidifies, forming an ocean ridge.

ISLAND CHAINS

When ocean plates collide, one plate subducts beneath the other. The volcanic activity which results from this may cause islands to break the ocean's surface and become visible. An example of an island chain formed in this way is the Lesser Antilles in the Caribbean (above).

The strength of an eruption depends on the types of magma and gases building up below the vent. When plates move apart, magma is runny. Gases in the magma escape gradually and the eruption is usually gentle. But where plates collide, thick magma is formed, which traps gases within it. They are released in a violent eruption.

ERUPTION !

Calm before the storm

Before its eruption in 1980, Mount St Helens had been dormant (inactive) since 1857.
Its snowy peak was a landmark for miles around. But warning signs in early May of 1980 showed that an eruption might be due: a small earthquake sent gas and steam into the air (above), and the side of the mountain bulged as magma rose below the cone.

ON CLOSER INSPECTION – *Peléean Eruption*

A Peléean eruption is the most explosive type of eruption. The name comes from the eruption of Mount Pelée on the Caribbean island of Martinique, in 1902. A hot cloud of lava, gas and ash poured on to the town of St Pierre (right), killing 38,000 people.

MOUNT ST HELENS

The eruption of Mount St Helens in the north-west United States in 1980 was one of the most violent in recent years. On 18 May an earthquake triggered a huge explosion which blew away the north side of the mountain, causing one of the worst landslides ever. Flows of rock, ash and gas cascaded down the mountain at terrifying speeds. Minutes later a second explosion threw a great column of ash and gas miles into the air (see left). The Mount St Helens eruption continued for four days, causing widespread devastation and killing 57 people. Sometimes the ash and gas expelled by an erupting volcano spills down the mountainsides in a *nuée ardente*, or glowing cloud. Such clouds may travel at speeds of more than 100kph, and are extremely dangerous. One such occurred when Mount Pelée erupted in 1902.

In a Hawaiian eruption, runny lava flows gradually from the vent to form a rounded shield volcano.

In a Strombolian eruption, fountains of ash, steam and gas pour from the cone. Lava bombs and chunks of rock are thrown into the air.

In a Peléean eruption, burning clouds of steam, gas and lava are blasted from the cone and pour down the sides of the volcano.

Nightlighting
Flying fragments of lava ejected by an erupting volcano show up as fiery traces when photographed at night.

L ava is red-hot, molten rock that flows from the crater of a volcano or oozes from the ground during an eruption. Lava flows are rarely dangerous, since they move slowly, often at only a few kilometres per hour. But, if the lava flow is large enough, it will spread across the countryside, causing destruction and engulfing towns and cities.

LIQUID

LAVA

When lava cools, it solidifies into two distinct formations. Scientists have not found any chemical difference between them. Their names are taken from Hawaiian words. *Aa* is slow-moving lava, which hardens into rough, crinkly shapes (below right). The sharp surface of a hardened *Aa* flow can tear shoes to ribbons. *Pahoehoe* lava is runny, fast-moving lava which solidifies to form a smooth skin, sometimes in long, ropey strands (below left).

ON CLOSER INSPECTION
– Collapsed Volcano

Once an eruption is over, the volcano's cone may collapse into the empty magma chamber below, forming a hollow caldera. Calderas often fill with water to form a lake (right).

ROCK

VOLCANIC BOMBS

If gases or water are present in lava during an eruption, fragments of rock may be hurled into the air. Volcanic blocks are pieces of hard, solid rock which are ejected during an eruption. Volcanic bombs are blobs of molten lava, which are sometimes twisted into strange shapes as they fly through the air.

Slow-moving, but deadly lava makes its way along a street in Hawaii.

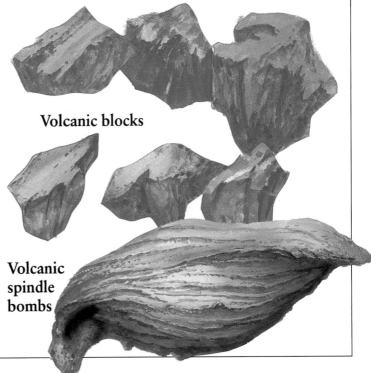

Volcanic blocks

Volcanic spindle bombs

An erupting volcano may expel great clouds of ash, made up of tiny fragments of rock which have been blown to pieces by the force of the explosion. In the hours after the eruption, ash thrown high in the air falls back to Earth in the region of the volcano burying fields and villages and causing further damage.

AFTER THE

Covered with ash

After the eruption of Mount St Helens in 1980, black ash fell over a wide area in the surrounding states of Washington, Oregon, Montana and Idaho. Towns more than 300 km away received 8 cm of ash. Around the volcano six million trees were flattened like matchsticks, and mudflows caused more destruction.

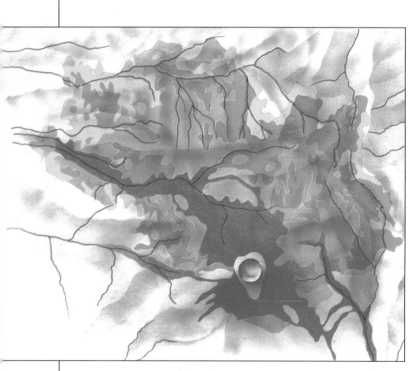

Tree blowdown areas (in orange)	Landslides	New lakes
Mudflow		Damaged trees

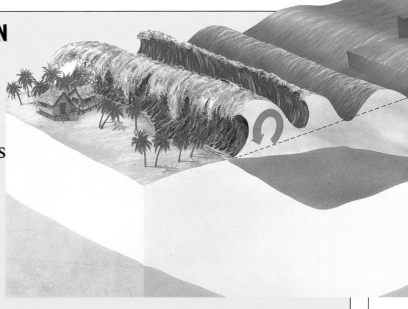

ON CLOSER INSPECTION – *Killer waves*

A *tsunami* is a giant tidal wave caused by an earthquake or by volcanic activity. It can travel across oceans at speeds of up to 800 kph, like a towering wall of water. In 1994 the Indonesian islands were hit by a series of *tsunamis* which swamped fields and villages.

ERUPTION

CHOKING ON ASH

Following the eruption of Mount Pinatubo in the Philippines in June 1991, villagers emerged to walk in a grey, ash-choked landscape (left). Some wore masks to protect their lungs from the ash; others without protection developed pneumonia – inflammation of the lungs.

WEATHER ALERT!

After an eruption, the surrounding area may experience high winds and torrential rain. The rain mixes with fallen ash, to cause dangerous flows of mud. After the eruption of Mount Pinatubo, mudflows engulfed roads, bridges and several villages (right).

One very famous eruption was that of Mt Vesuvius, Italy, in AD 79. The Roman town of Pompeii, which lay beneath the volcano, was engulfed by flows of ash and mud which preserved the town, up until excavations began in the 18th century. Today these towns are a record of everyday life in ancient Italy.

VOLCANOES

Vesuvius erupts

Before its eruption Vesuvius had been dormant for hundreds of years. The Romans thought it was extinct. They were terrified when glowing clouds buried Pompeii in two metres of ash, killing 20,000 residents. As the clouds engulfed the city people were buried in layers of ash which set around their bodies and turned to rock. The bodies decayed to form hollows in the rock. In the 1860s a method was invented to form lifelike casts of those who had been buried (above).

KRAKATAU

One of the most violent eruptions in history occurred on the uninhabited island of Krakatau in Indonesia in 1883. The island was destroyed and *tsunamis* drowned 36,000 people on the neighbouring islands of Java and Sumatra.

The sound of the explosion was heard in Australia, nearly 5,000 km away.

The legend of Atlantis, a city lost under the sea, was probably inspired by an eruption on the Greek island of Thera, now Santorini, around 1470 BC. The eruption destroyed the Minoan civilisation living on Crete.

IN HISTORY

ST PIERRE

Another of the worst volcanic disasters in modern times was the destruction of the port of St Pierre on the Caribbean island of Martinique, in 1902 (right). When Mount Pelée erupted, the town was overtaken in minutes by a burning cloud of ash and gas. Only one of the port's 38,000 inhabitants survived, and that was only because he was protected by the thick walls of the town gaol.

Original photograph of devastation to the port of St Pierre.

During a major volcanic explosion, lots of gases are released into the atmosphere. These include carbon dioxide and sulphur dioxide. Gases from volcanoes have always contributed to the balanced mixture of gases which make up the atmosphere. Nowadays, however, these volcanic gases may add to the harmful effects of man-made pollution, increasing environmental problems for the Earth.

Crops at risk

Farmers who work fields near volcanoes welcome light falls of volcanic ash. They fertilise the soil and give bumper harvests. Heavy ashfalls, however, destroy crops. The photo above, taken after the eruption of Mount Pinatubo, shows a heavy ashfall engulfing a crop.

VOLCANO

The picture below shows dust from the eruption of Mount Pinatubo spreading around the area.

CLIMATE PROBLEMS

Some eruptions are powerful enough to affect the weather, and even the climate on a global scale. Clouds of ash (below left) thrown high into the air by a volcano may reach the stratosphere, high in the Earth's atmosphere. Strong winds carry the dust particles around the world, causing spectacular sunrises and sunsets. The false colour satellite image (right) shows sulphur dioxide released by the eruption of Mount Pinatubo spreading across the globe. The white area is the sulphur dioxide.

ON CLOSER INSPECTION
– Erupting Giant
The eruption of Mt Tambora in Indonesia in 1815 was the largest recorded eruption. Dust particles spread around the world, causing summer frosts and snow in Europe and Scandinavia. This watercolour by the artist JMW Turner shows a spectacular sunset caused by this volcanic dust.

HAZARDS

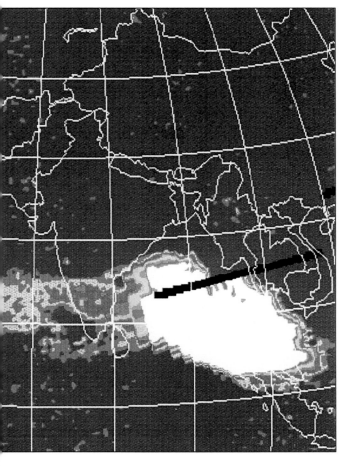

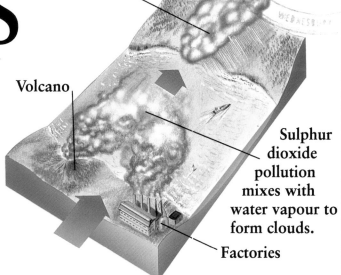

Acid rain

Volcano

Sulphur dioxide pollution mixes with water vapour to form clouds.

Factories

ACID RAIN
Sulphur dioxide from volcanoes also increases the problem of acid rain. Acid rain (above) is caused by sulphur dioxide and nitrogen oxides in the air. When it mixes with water vapour in the air, it forms a very weak acid. This acid then falls to the ground in the form of rain, snow or dust. This acid deposition can kill trees, destroy buildings and poison life in ponds, rivers and lakes.

Hot, hot, hot
Long metal rods are used to collect samples of red-hot lava and to measure the depth of lava flows.

Of the 500 active volcanoes in the world, between 20 and 30 erupt each year. Recording volcanic activity and trying to predict eruptions is done by vulcanologists. Some of this is done on computers, from the safety of the laboratory. Other work must be done on site, at great risk to the people involved.

EXPERTS AT

Sea discovery
It is hard for scientists to study undersea volcanoes. So deep-sea trenches are explored in small submarines called submersibles (below). This one is a robot submersible which doesn't need scientists on board to operate it.

ON CLOSER INSPECTION
– Into the Inferno
Mount Erebus is the only active volcano in Antarctica. The machine shown here, named *Dante*, was built to carry out tests and monitor activity inside this particular volcano's crater.

WORK

ALL SUITED UP
Working at the volcano, scientists take samples of ash and lava, measure lava temperatures and monitor the exact shape of the volcano. Vulcanologists can use an electric thermometer called a thermocouple to record the temperature of lava. Molten lava can reach temperatures of more than 1,000 degrees centigrade. If they work very close to the volcano, special suits may be needed to protect the experts from fumes, extreme heat and other dangers. The suits are made of fireproof material which reflects the heat. Heavy helmets help protect the head from small pieces of falling rock, and masks screen out dangerous gases and dust. Asbestos gloves are worn to protect the hands from the searing heat.

DANGEROUS OCCUPATIONS
Maurice and Katia Krafft were a French husband and wife team of vulcanologists who spent their lives studying volcanoes. They were so passionate about their field of study that news of an eruption would send them racing for the first plane to the stricken region. Together they witnessed many eruptions. Both were killed during the eruption of Mt Unzen in Japan in 1991 (below) when they were engulfed by glowing clouds.

Emergency aid
Rescuers carry a survivor of the mudslides at Armero, in South America. These mudslides occured in 1985 after an earthquake.

Millions of people in the world live close enough to volcanoes to be at great risk should the volcano erupt. Most settle so close to farm the land with its fertile soil, which has formed from volcanic rock through centuries of erosion. Scientists study volcanic activity hoping to reduce the dangers to people from volcanoes, but some eruptions are still unpredictable.

LIVING IN

MUD – THE ENEMY
Mudslides and avalanches are a major danger for those living in the volcano's shadow. In 1985, the volcano Nevado del Ruiz, in Colombia, South America, erupted. Ice and snow melted by the lava transformed ash from the eruption into flows of mud which engulfed villages and towns on the lower slopes of the mountain. The town of Armero (see left) 50 km away was buried by a mudflow 40 m deep and 20,000 people died.

ON CLOSER INSPECTION
– Active, dormant, extinct?

Dormant volcanoes are those that have not erupted for many years (bottom). A volcano that has not erupted for thousands of years is said to be extinct (middle). But some "extinct" volcanoes surprise the experts and suddenly erupt. One of the most active volcanoes (top) is Mt Bromo in Java.

FEAR?

PEOPLE AGAINST NATURE

Vulcanologists use various methods to try to control the direction of mud- and lava flows. On Mt Etna in Sicily in 1983 experts used dynamite in an attempt to construct a channel to divert lava flows into a nearby crater (left). Japan, on the Pacific Ring of Fire (page 9), has a large population and many active volcanoes. On the slopes of some volcanoes there, dams have been built to protect the settlements below from mudflows.

olcanoes benefit humans in many ways. Lava flows form and change the landscape. Also, volcanic soil is fertile for growing crops and grazing herds, and volcanic activity can also be harnessed to provide heat and power. Many different kinds of rocks are made by volcanic activity. These are calle igneous rocks.

VOLCANO –

Energy sources

Heat from volcanoes is harnessed to produce geothermal energy (energy from the Earth) in countries such as Iceland, New Zealand and Japan. Hot rocks underground heat groundwater which gives off steam (above). Steam is tapped to produce electricity at geothermal stations (below). About 40 per cent of Iceland's electricity comes from geothermal energy. Farmers can even grow bananas there, thanks to the use of geothermal heat, which creates the right climate.

BUMPER CROP

In many parts of the world farmers benefit from rich volcanic soils to grow crops. Many fruits grow well on volcanic slopes in the Canary Islands, north-west of Africa. The soils around Mount Etna are ideal for growing oranges, lemons and grapes for wine. Rice is cultivated in terraced fields on the slopes of volcanoes in Bali, Indonesia (below).

ON CLOSER INSPECTION
– Life after Death

After lava or ash has covered a landscape, it may take years or even centuries for plants to grow again. Plants take root more quickly in ash than in lava. But, unusually, in Hawaii (right) mosses and ferns may root in new lava in less than a year.

FRIEND OR FOE?

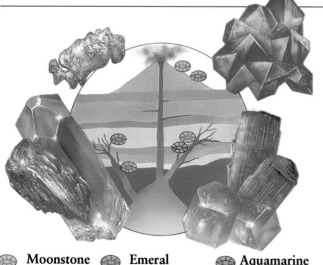

| Moonstone | Emeral | Aquamarine |
| Zircon | Topaz | Tourmaline |

IGNEOUS ROCKS

Igneous rocks (below) include granite, formed when magma cools as the continental crust cools, and basalt, formed when lava cools. Granite is a hard, coarse-grained rock often used for building houses and churches. Walls and kerbstones are often made of granite. Other minerals formed by volcanic activity include sulphur and pumice (which contains gas bubbles). It is so light it can float on water.

GEMSTONES

Valuable minerals and gemstones such as opals and sapphires are also found in volcanic rock. Gold, silver and copper are mined near some extinct volcanoes in South Africa.

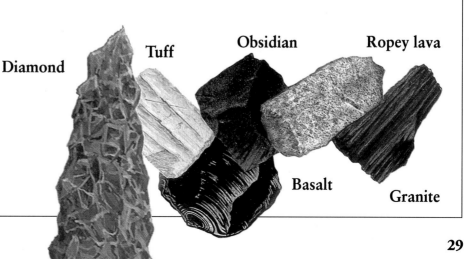

Diamond

Tuff

Obsidian

Ropey lava

Basalt

Granite

AD 79 Mt Vesuvius in southern Italy erupts, burying the inhabitants (above), of Pompeii and Herculaneum in flows of ash and mud.

Loa (below rght), in Hawaii erupts for 18 months.

1883 Explosive eruption on the island of Krakatau, Indonesia, causes *tsunamis* which drown 36,000 people. The explosion is heard as far away as Australia and Madagascar.

1902 Eruption of Mount Pelée on the island of Martinique in the Caribbean

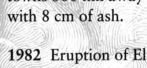

CHRONOLOGY OF MAJOR ERUPTIONS

1669 Mount Etna (above right), in Sicily erupts killing about 20,000 people.

1783 Eruptions of Skaftar in Iceland and Asama in Japan cause a "Little Ice Age" in Europe, and lower the temperatures around the world.

1815 Eruption of Mt Tambora, Indonesia, is the largest recorded in history, emitting 80 cubic kilometres of ash and killing more than 90,000 people.

1855-1856 The world's largest volcano, Mauna

causes glowing clouds to blast the port of St Pierre, wiping out all but one of the town's 38,000 inhabitants.

1943 Birth of a volcano in a farmer's field in Paracutin, Mexico. The volcano remains active until 1952, reaching a height of 2,700 m.

1963 Birth of the volcanic island of Surtsey near Iceland.

1980 Mount St Helens in north-west USA erupts with a massive explosion, showering

towns 300 km away with 8 cm of ash.

1982 Eruption of El Chichon in Mexico darkens the sky for 44 hours and kills 3,500 people.

1985 Eruption of Nevado del Ruiz in Colombia, causes mudflows to engulf the town of Armero 50 km away, killing 20,000 inhabitants.

1991 Eruption of Mt Unzen in Japan kills 38 people, including vulcanologists Maurice and Katia Krafft.

1991 Mt Pinatubo in the Philippines erupts without warning, emitting 7 cubic km of ash.

1994 Eruption near Rabaul, Papua New Guinea, showers the town with 1 m of ash.

1996 Eruption of Mt Rua Petu in New Zealand. It is an ash-based eruption with almost no lava flows. Over 3 m of ash covers a vast area, causing roofs to collapse. There are no casualties.

Aa Lava which has hardened with a rough, spikey surface.

Active Describes a volcano that may erupt at any time.

Black smoker Hot volcanic spring formed on a mid-ocean ridge, releasing clouds of water black with minerals.

Caldera Huge crater formed when the sides of a volcano collapse.

Core The centre of the Earth, a ball of intensely hot metal.

Crater Funnel-shaped opening at the top of a volcano.

Crust Hardened outer layer of the Earth's surface.

Dormant Describes a volcano that has not erupted for a long time, but may become active again.

Emit To release or give off. Erupting volcanoes emit ash, steam and gases as well as lava.

Extinct Describes a volcano which has not erupted for thousands of years, and which experts do not believe will erupt again.

Geothermal energy Energy that comes from heat inside the Earth.

Glowing cloud Cloud of burning ash and gas released by an erupting volcano. Glowing clouds are highly dangerous.

Hotspot volcano Volcano that has formed in the middle of a plate, over a source of magma.

Igneous rock Rock formed when lava or magma cools and hardens.

Lava Magma from inside the Earth that has erupted on the Earth's surface.

Magma Molten rock inside the Earth.

Magma chamber Place below a volcano which fills with hot magma.

GLOSSARY

Mantle Layer of semi-molten rock that lies between the Earth's crust and the core.

Pahoehoe Lava which has hardened with a smooth surface.

Pillow lava Lava that erupts underwater.

Plate A section of the Earth's crust.

Pumice Light volcanic rock filled with bubbles of gas.

Tsunami Giant wave caused by an earthquake or volcano.

Vent Passage leading from the volcano's magma chamber to the Earth's surface, through which gas, steam, ash and lava may escape.

Vulcanologist A scientist who studies volcanoes.

INDEX

Photo Credits

Abbreviations: t-top, m-middle, b-bottom, r-right, l-left.
All the pictures in this book are supplied by Frank Spooner pictures except the following pages: 7 & 23b - Science Photo Library. 9 & 29 - James Davis Travel Photography. 15, 21, 30tl & 30 background - Hulton Getty Collection. 23 - Tate Gallery Publications. 25t - NASA. 28b - Eye Ubiquitous.